TURN LIFE'S LEMONS INTO MILKSHAKES

*The Art of Manifesting Your Dreams
and Handling Success*

Flynt Flossy

Turn Life's Lemons into Milkshakes: The Art of Manifesting Your Dreams and Handling Success

Book and Cover illustration by Aria Feliciano

ISBN: 978-1-7330839-1-1

Contents

1

Talk to Your Spirit and Speak with Your Actions; You're Closer to Your Dreams than You Think

SO WHAT'S YOUR DEFINITION OF SUCCESS? Take a moment to really think about it, I'll wait...I know right, it's so relative, but it's all about perception. Ok, check this: The achievements in your life that you neglect are what someone else may be wishing for. So, when you really put things in perspective and view it from an objective eye, you are already successful or damn closer than you think, feel me? Now, how you measure your own success solely depends on you. If you keep comparing yourself to "Flaunting Fred and Showoff Shelly" on social media, the people who always portray a worry-free life, you may always find yourself chasing and trying to play catch-up. Good luck ever finding spiritual fulfillment doing that type of shit.

Are you able to do what you love? Are you affecting other lives? These are important questions to ask yourself.

So, when I say you're already successful, am I saying this to make you feel like you've already made it and you should stop striving for new levels? Nah, it's me saying don't take for granted all you have already accomplished on your journey.

It's crazy how powerful the mind is, the art of believing can sometimes be underestimated. You have to truly understand that all the vision boards in your room don't mean shit if you don't believe it enough to manifest. I'm not saying if you close your eyes, click your heels together, and wish hard enough, all your desires will magically appear. I'm saying you have to believe hard enough to take action. That picture of your dream home glued to your vision board will only come into fruition if you are willing to work hard enough for it.

There is great power in our thoughts; people can often psyche themselves out of pursuing an idea by overthinking; always waiting for "the perfect time." But really, when is the perfect time? Why not wear those shoes that have been collecting dust in your closet for years? Fuck a special occasion, stop thinking so hard and put them on now. The obstacles people envision between the points of start and finish discourages them from even starting the race. But the small steps lead to big results. Once you begin moving forward, whatever your pace is will be faster than the words "never started."

Say if you dreamed of writing a book, start by creating a new document on your computer. Even if you have no clue on what it will be about, save it as "my completed project," that's called taking a step towards manifestation. That's exactly what I did, and here we are today, you're reading my published book. This is the mentality you need in order to overcome life's obstacles and just make shit happen. Ask yourself, "Is that fire burning inside of me worth chasing?" If so, then it can happen! Now, it's just a matter of how you will handle it when it actually does manifest.

For all those reading this and wondering, who the hell is this dude? My name is Flynt Flossy; my fans also know me as, F dot Floss Internatioknown...baybee! I'm a music producer, filmmaker, writer, entrepreneur, and I guess whatever else you choose to consider me after reading this book. I'm just a dude that likes creating shit. Like any other man, I'm still pushing forward and always striving for new heights. But that doesn't discredit what I have already achieved, and you should feel the same way about yourself. As I said earlier, sometimes we get so caught up with where we want to be, we neglect where we've already been, feel me?

I was able to manifest my dreams by turning my pain into motivation. Constant rejection throughout my life forced me to be innovative. I believe the famous saying is, "When life gives you lemons, make lemonade." Well, when life gave me lemons, I had to go above and beyond and make milkshakes. I had to think outside the box and do what was unexpected. I knew I had to create my own opportunities because people rarely gave me chances. A thought in my head would eventually become a reality and turn into a platform that acquired millions of viewers worldwide along with a loyal growing fan base. I have seen places I thought I'd never see as a child growing up in the hood. It still trips me out that an idea I had would eventually become a livelihood for fellow like-minds and myself. Let's be clear, I'm no different from you. I actually believe you are already where you want to be or damn near close. In fact, I'm so confident about it that in this book, among other topics, I will discuss what you can expect with the success you're destined for. I will talk about the unexpected situations I encountered on my journey and my mental/spiritual approaches to them. You can use my words to aid in your preparation or just to simply reflect.

What I speak is only my truth, my viewpoints based on what I've personally experienced or witnessed, and the obstacles I faced. So, whether you agree or disagree with my insight, I want your thoughts to be provoked. I want you to break through any mental barriers you've created in your mind and reach new heights beyond expectations. I want you to know that you're not alone in whatever you're going or been through. Hopefully, you can either relate or learn from my lessons, but most importantly grow.

2

Story of the Man Behind the Shades

I was a child raised in the arts, the type of kid that always had principal roles in his grade school plays. I even auditioned for a film or two and did some theater in Harlem, New York. But you know what? For me, it was never about the attention, I don't yearn for people to recognize me on the street and swoon, it was always about the art. So, whether I'm behind the scenes or in the forefront, evoking feeling from a person can be euphoric. If I bring someone joy or provoke their thoughts, to know it was because of my art is a feeling I can't describe.

I grew up in New York City, the Bronx to be exact. It was a rough time, but a strong family support system kept my head on straight. My parents were immigrants from Ghana in West Africa, and as far as I remember, they've always worked incredibly hard to give my three older brothers and I a better life. My mom came home at late hours from working double shifts as a registered nurse. And my father initially worked as a cook to put himself through school. He eventually obtained a business degree and became a social worker.

Whenever times got rough, my parents never made it noticeable. I never knew the power was off because of a past due bill, I just thought having candles lit around a dark house was a sexy way to do homework. No matter the circumstance, my parents always had this energy of "everything will turn out fine, if you just keep pushing." It made me realize at an early age you have to believe in yourself before anyone else does. Create your own opportunities if they're not given.

No matter how many of my father's business ideas fell through, he still had this fire that couldn't be extinguished, which was so inspiring to me. Every 10 months, it was always, "Son, I have a new business idea!" Whether it was starting a janitorial service company or selling traditional African garbs out of a closet, it was always something. These persistent values became instilled in me; even as a kid, I knew I needed to work hard because the world wouldn't give me shit easy.

Growing up in the Bronx was wild. At the age of five, I became used to seeing junkies get high as I walked home from school with my big brother. I was desensitized to hearing gunshots at night and seeing prostitutes negotiate with potential clients near the house I first lived. Eventually, we were able to move to an area of the Bronx that wasn't as terrible, but it wasn't a cakewalk either.

Creating would become an escape for me; at an early age, I would make rocket ships out of old cardboard boxes my aunt would bring home, and build fortresses out of my mom's encyclopedia book sets, then stage civil wars with my homemade foil men. It was great for my imagination, but all the wasted aluminum was costly for my frugal father.

As I entered my teenage years, while friends were being introduced to gang life, I was writing short stories, watching anime, creating songs and dissecting music videos; but, most of all, I was dancing. The way I learned how to dance seemed like divine destiny. It wasn't the traditional route like taking dance classes as a toddler or attending a performing arts school.

One summer, I got an eye injury playing street football. The doctor ordered me not to expose my eye to sunlight, so I was basically stuck in the house for two months. I then had all day to teach myself how to dance by watching music videos. So yeah, seemed like it was meant to happen.

Dancing immediately became a love for me and being known as "the guy that can dance his ass off," definitely had its perks in the neighborhood. Fresh moves plus a charming personality was a good combo to attract the ladies. Nothing like having a girl write her number on your hand because she's enamored by how you moonwalk down the school halls. It was an absolute chick magnet, and women would become an early weakness for me. I was that dude in high school who always had campfire stories around his locker; my lady tales had my friends in suspense, asking questions like, "She did what?! Wow, you the man! And then what happened?!"

I'll tell you one thing – I could never master the art of "not getting caught." One too many times, I had a girlfriend tell me, "You think I don't already know you're messing with that bitch! All my friends been seen you!" As I reflect on those situations, I'm reminded of how terrible I was at lying.

People around the neighborhood had a different kind of respect for me; they respected the fact that I was true to myself. In an environment that was violent, I never tried to be a gangster. Of course, it was virtually impossible to avoid trouble at times; every day, I had to walk past one of the worst housing projects in New York to get to school. I've had guns drawn on me and got into plenty fights mainly defending friends and myself, but regardless, I wasn't a follower. I was never a kid that did bad shit for the sake of impressing people. When I walked past gang members on the way home, they would say, "I know him, he cool! Let him through, he don't fuck with nobody." They would even go as far as defending me if I had problems.

However, even though I got respect, at the same time, I was constantly ridiculed mainly for my dark skin tone. "You're so black, you can leave fingerprints on charcoal" and "you're so black, I bet you bleed smoke" are the types of cruel comments I would endure growing up. There were people that treated my melanin like a disease. I recall a time in grade school, a friend telling me I could no longer come by his house to play videogames because his mom said my dark skin creeped her out. As a child, I had to learn to be quick on my feet with comeback jokes because people teased me so bad. I would eventually develop an "I just don't give a fuck" type of attitude, which ironically made people gravitate to my personality even more. Everyone would often tell me how hilarious I was without me giving effort, but I was honestly just being myself.

In addition to the derogatory remarks on my skin tone, some people would also tell me my passion for dancing was a waste of time. I would always hear remarks like, "You still doing that corny shit? You're not going anywhere with that bullshit, give it up, bruh!" However, I never did let those kinds of comments deter me. I loved dancing too much, and it was my therapy. Whether it was on a street corner in Manhattan in front of spectators or talent shows at a local youth center, I was always performing.

On warm summer nights, I would attend backyard parties in the neighborhood, crowds would say, "Oh shit he's here!" and clear the floor for me. Dancing was my solace, and I didn't care about doubtful outside opinions, as it was my ticket out of the hood.

When I graduated from high school, my mom was concerned that I, her youngest of four boys, planned to move away from home to pursue his dreams and an education. You see, when I was 11 years old, one of my older brothers was found dead in a New York City subway. There weren't any witnesses, so we never knew the exact details of how he fell to his death, he could have been murdered. That uncertainty was always painful for us. It hurt being shrouded in such mystery, but it also hurt too much to keep asking questions.

Since that tragic day, my mom became exceedingly protective of her children. She made it a habit of calling all my friends' houses when I didn't come home at a certain hour. On many occasions, I had to channel my inner Spider-Man and climb my way in and out the 3rd story bathroom window, in order to spend late nights with a high school fling. I swore my plan was surefire until she began noticing my sneaker prints in the bathtub. The last time I attempted my ninja-like bathroom entrance, she surprised me at the window with a hard smack across my face. "You must really think I'm stupid!" she shouted. But I couldn't be mad, she was just a mother that loved her son that much, till this day she reminds me to lock my doors and not take candy from strangers.

But no matter how worried she seemed to be, it never affected her support. Both she and my dad would always say, "I'll love whatever you decide to do." Our happiness was most important to them, and I will forever be appreciative. The love of my family emboldened me, and that support was vital for the journey ahead. I knew it was time to get out and chase my dreams. I wanted to take my talents beyond backyard party circles and local talent shows.

When I left home and arrived in a new city, I had nothing but high hopes in mind. I was so naïve, greener than a granny smith apple. Pursuing a career in dance was my passion, but the politics involved was a rude awakening. Between not knowing "the right people" and me not having "the right look," I barely got booked. People would always tell me how amazing my style was, but I could never get a gig.

I remember one particular time I spent my last $4 on gas to get to a dance audition. According to the flyer, I snagged a day earlier; they were in search of popping freestylers for an upcoming music video. "This is right up my alley!" I said to myself. I waited three hours in line, and when it was my turn up, a woman from the judges' table wearing dark sunglasses and her hat low shouted in a cocky tone, "NOPE...NEXT!" as she sipped her morning cappuccino. I was speechless; *I didn't even get to dance?* Talk about some soul-crushing shit!

I became discouraged from all the rejection I endured, and to top that, I was super broke. I was broke like one of those busted cheap leg lamps you find at local garage sales. I remember how excited I was to hear Popeye's Chicken had a "3 biscuits for a dollar" deal. Let's just say for a while I lived off of biscuits and occasional home-cooked meals from women who fancied me.

My residence was a friend's couch at this point, and no matter how cool he was about me staying there, it still killed my spirits. I hated feeling like a burden. I was stressed out beyond belief, unsure of my life's direction. Also, the girl I was in love with back in the Bronx abruptly ended our long-distance relationship for another man. I can't say I was completely innocent in the matter, the mental strain from my career or lack thereof made me distant. Our late-night phone calls became more and more seldom. I neglected her, and it broke her heart. "I'm dumping you because I feel like I'm #2! You forgot about me!" she cried. But it wasn't another woman stealing my attention, I was only trying to find myself. But it was too late when I tried to explain my side; she was already fed up. "YOU not paying attention to me made it easier for another guy to fuck me! It's YOUR fault!" she said to me. My throat tightened, I felt my heart escort itself out my chest and crawl into the nearest wastebasket.

If the goal of her ice-cold tone was to crush my feelings, it damn sure worked. I was the only man she was intimate with up until that point. It took me two years of courting before she was ready to have sex, but it only took a matinee movie date and a shopping spree at Old Navy for another guy to sign his name on her panties. This coochie crook stole my girl, and I was pissed! The image of her in ecstasy with another man kept replaying in my head. I briefly picked up the habit of smoking in an attempt to ease the pain; I would smoke my friends' leftover cigarettes when

I couldn't afford my own pack. I needed a way to get my mind off it all.

It was imperative I compose myself and get focused. I knew if my father or older brothers caught wind that a girl had my head so twisted, I wouldn't hear the end of it. I can hear my father in his strong West African accent now, "WHAT! MY SON IS CRYING OVER A GAL?" I couldn't let my broken heart distract me, so I man'd up and pushed forward. I had other things to worry about; I was virtually on the verge of homelessness, and I had to figure out how to get my life in order.

My pockets were so hurt I began to consider doing things out my character. I had a friend or two that were big-time dope dealers; they offered me a way into the lifestyle so I could create some income. I thought long and hard about it and kept telling myself, "Ok, I'm just getting in and getting the fuck out. I can't possibly get caught? I won't do it for long!" I wasn't, in any way, the money-hungry type; I could care less about making it rain dollars at the strip club or pulling up to a ritzy lounge in the latest foreign car to impress some pretentious assholes standing outside. All I wanted was enough money to pay my bills and enough free time to pursue my dancing dream.

However, my thoughts of considering the illegal life were extremely short-lived. I remember the feeling of anxiety when I saw a blueberry-colored Mercedes Benz pull up next to me in a deserted parking lot, slowly roll down his tinted windows, and say in a semi-deep voice, "You the dude I'm supposed to meet? You got the product?" A dull pain in the pit of my stomach told me immediately that this would be my first and last day in the dealer business; it just wasn't me. Who the hell was I kidding? I couldn't even juggle multiple girlfriends in high school effectively; I'd make a terrible dope dealer.

Additionally, my parents worked too hard to get me to this point. You see, they're big on integrity. In Ghana, my mom holds the title *Queen Mother* of her hometown; it's a royal ranking that represents power and leadership. And my father is heavily involved in politics, always fighting for social injustices. So even though I wasn't rich monetarily growing up, my parents were adamant about their children being rich in honor.

It would crush their hearts if I ever had to call them from a jail cell because I got busted pushing some dope. Also, they would proceed in crushing my ass. My mom had a mean left hook I wanted no parts of. There had to be another way for me to make money.

I was forced to sacrifice the time I devoted to dance auditions and creative writing in order to make some funds. I picked up several jobs from selling newspapers at a call center to bar backing and occasionally cleaning toilets at a nightclub. I even built displays at convention centers from time to time. It all was extremely strenuous, and it didn't help that my car was less reliable than a refurbished toaster. Yeah, I had little free time, but at least I slept better than I would if I took the illegal route I briefly considered.

But no matter the number of jobs I had, I always found a way to devote any window of free time to my passions. I joined forces with other fellow dancers I met on my journey and put together my own performance troupe. We had dance showcases on college campuses and conventions around the city. This got my name buzzing in the industry; I soon became "that dude you had to see dance!" Soon, underground and mainstream artists were coming to me for choreography and artist development. I would always hear "you're the guy I keep hearing about!" when first meeting people. Things started to pick up, and my name was getting around as a choreographer, but I still felt I wasn't where I wanted to be. Between multiple part-time jobs and school, I was still breaking my back just to make a buck.

One warm spring day on my way to class, a bright sign leaned against a table caught my attention. It read:

Make a 5-minute short film! We will provide the equipment! All for FREE!

It sounded a little too good to be true. I thought it was some sort of scam to get my email address, so I could be spammed with free psychic readings and credit card offers. But no, it was absolutely real! The man at the table assured me that they were a traveling film festival that offered students free equipment to produce a short film in seven days. The timing was surreal; at this point in my life, the dance industry had taken a toll on me mentally. On top of that, I'm always writing songs and short stories, so writing a film script makes sense!

It was a grueling process, as this was my first time shooting a short film, and it was way harder than I expected. Between casting, shooting, locations, and editing, I remember thinking aloud, "Damn, this shit is hard as hell," but you know what? I developed a love for the process; it was extremely refreshing finding another creative outlet.

The night my film premiered plays vividly in my head. It was a packed auditorium; people stood at all corners of the room just to get a glimpse of the films playing on the massive screen. Then, finally, it was my turn. The opening scene faded in, and as my film began playing, I remember seeing the faces of people in the audience. I was in awe, something that I created from scratch was evoking all these different emotions from people, this shit is wild! The adrenaline rush was comparable to me performing on stage.

As soon as my film ended, I received a standing ovation, it was placed in the top 3. Was I ecstatic? Hell yeah! But I was even more excited to discover another way to creatively express myself, and at that very moment, I officially fell in love with filmmaking.

With the discovery of my newfound passion, I felt rejuvenated, the sky's the limit and nothing could stop me. I stopped attending a radio DJ internship I had at the time and began studying under a highly regarded film professor in the industry. "Promise me you'll always keep at it. I truly believe in you," he would tell me. His inspiring words fueled my fire and reinforced my decision to focus on the new title added to my description...filmmaker. I found a new life, I thought to myself, *There couldn't possibly be as many politics as the dance industry, right?* ...WRONG, I was so wrong.

I picked up another side job, and used every penny I earned to buy my own camera and editing equipment. I then created several short films, spent years producing and shooting a full-length independent feature I wrote, and spent long nights crafting my video editing skills. I even volunteered my services for a special program at the Cannes France film festival, just so I could learn about different techniques in film while working out there. Attempt after attempt, and no matter how often I heard someone say, "Your style is so uniquely incredible. I've never seen anything like it!" I rarely got into film festivals because I didn't know the "right people." I didn't have a fancy agent nor the necessary connections, stupid politics once again!

So, there I was, a heartbroken kid from the hood that thought all he needed was his talent to carry him through. But I was experiencing the same hardships as a filmmaker as I was as a dancer, so it's all the same bullshit. I was emotionally drained; my inner spirit sedan broke down at a dead-end street on no-hope road.

One hot sunny day, I lay on the floor staring at the ceiling. The film, *Eternal Sunshine of the Spotless Mind* played on repeat in my DVD player because the cable bill was past due. I just got finished arguing on the phone with some dickhead from the student loan office that felt he had something to prove. Apparently, they wanted my kidney and left testicle as monthly payments, at least that's what it felt like. I also just received another film festival rejection letter. It read, "Thanks for your entry! Unfortunately, at this time your film hasn't been selected. We hope that you blah blah blah yada yada..."

I shouted out of frustration. "WHAT THE FUCK?? I don't get it?? I just can't get a break!"

I felt low as shit, I hit rock bottom mentally and emotionally. It felt like I had been taking a whole lot of risks with no reward. I was drowning in a pool of self-doubt. I thought to myself, *What if it never happens for me? What will I do next? What's my purpose?* I knew it wasn't healthy to remain in this state of mind. I prayed and meditated for hours, as I knew it was important to get back in tune with my mind and spirit. I couldn't keep feeling sorry for myself like some sucker.

Rain pattered on the window that night as I reflected deeply. *Ok, I don't have a fancy agent to make the right calls or a major investor to pay the right people. But this is the hand I was dealt. So, I can either work with what I have and be great or keep moping around like a sucker.* I immediately felt something call to my spirit. I grabbed a cue card from my backpack, and I began writing a contract to myself. I vowed that I would create something. I had no clue what this something was yet, but it would inspire people. It would carve a path for others who can relate to the way I feel. I was sick and tired of all this politics bullshit! I can be the anomaly and make a difference. My moment of self-doubt subsequently subsided. I knew I had to snap out of it and keep it moving, keep creating. I grabbed a handful of my nuts and threw out the pity porridge. Fuck that feeling sorry for myself shit.

At this point, my mindset was reformed, and I also realized I couldn't hold a regular job if it were glued to my hands. The cubicle life just wasn't my thing even if it was part-time. Co-workers would always express how much they loved my presence, but at the same time encourage me to leave so I can fully commit to pursuing my passions. "Why are you here? I don't want to see you go, but this job really isn't you!" I would often hear.

So, one afternoon, I disconnected my headset in mid-conversation with a customer and stood up from my cubicle. I strolled into the break room, grabbed my half-eaten chicken calzone from the communal fridge and walked out. I told myself that moving forward all of my income will be directly or indirectly related to my passions. So, something like doing videography for a baby shower wouldn't be ideal for me, but it beats being stuck on the phone and getting cursed out by some cranky 73-year old man for trying to sell him newspaper subscriptions at eight in the morning.

I began putting my skills to use and made ends meet by doing video production for whoever was paying. One week, I'm cutting footage of a dog show and the next I'm color-correcting the thong of a stripper named Caramel Cream for an adult entertainment website. I revised the reels of local actors, did some photography and occasionally freelanced as a scriptwriter. I also developed a working relationship with that traveling film festival that gave me my start in filmmaking.

Shooting music videos for up and coming musicians became a key source of income for me as well. I became the guy artists would come to if they didn't have a major label budget, but they still needed top quality with my signature twist.

Between new clients and my personal projects, I stayed busy. In addition to that, I picked up a pretty consistent gig being an MCEE and dancer at Bar Mitzvahs. Yeah, I was a random black dude shouting "Hava Nagila" on the microphone while partaking in the Hora dance. At this stage of my life, I wasn't exactly where I wanted to be, but I was in a much better place than before. At least I wasn't as broke and my income was either directly or indirectly related to my passions. I was able to move from my friend's couch to an apartment with a roommate and upgrade from Popeye's biscuits to actual groceries.

One evening, I was at my wits' end with a particular client. The slippery son of a bitch tried to weasel his way out of payment for some video work I did. Tired and aggravated, I just needed a break from all the frustration; I needed another creative way to relieve stress besides sporadic nights of intimacy with a lady friend. Then it came to me, *I'm using my skills to do music videos for all these artists; why not invest in myself as an artist? This way I'd have no one to answer to, no one to say, "I need you to change this and adjust that."*

The wheels in my head began turning. My plan was to create a song with an accompanying video and give absolutely NO fucks about the content or the aesthetics. I wanted to produce whatever came to my head and not care about consequences; it would serve as my therapy. I mean, why not? We are in a time where the Internet enables you to take matters into your own hands. I can just create it, upload it, and see what happens.

Excited about my epiphany, I first brought the idea to my close friend who'd later become my business partner. I figured he would be hesitant at first. After all, he was a trained musician and something this unorthodox may be intimidating.

"You want me to do what???" he said. Yup, he was hesitant as I anticipated, but he was also the real supportive type. The kind of guy that would do anything for his friends. He gave me a baffled stare, but then said, "Ok, fuck it, let's do it...but I don't want people to recognize me!" I assured him we would be incognito once we threw on some dark shades. Funny thing is, I felt the same way he did. It's not that I was ashamed or anything, but I rather have people concentrate on the art of it all, it wasn't about me.

Within a week of presenting him the idea, we created a song on his old microphone and dated desktop. The song was entitled, *Stretchy Pants,* and it was about our admiration for women who wore spandex. I know what you're thinking, "Huh??? Random???" but as I stated earlier this was a time of therapy. I wanted to produce whatever was on my mind and give zero fucks if it made sense to anyone else. So yes, at that particular time the beauty of women in spandex was on our brain.

When the song was completed, shooting the visual soon followed. It wasn't an easy task explaining the vision to the women who were cast in the video, but we eventually got it done.

I can truly say I felt liberated while editing the footage. I wasn't confined by certain rules or instructions assigned to me. It was a sense of freedom; granted there was a method to the madness, but now I wasn't worried about being too abstract. My feelings were comparable to Pablo Picasso throwing paint on a canvas and not caring where it lands. I found myself losing track of time as I sat in my bed sipping on peppermint tea and meticulously putting together each shot on my lucky laptop. It was a tedious process, especially being my struggling laptop was on its last leg and would shut off every so often. But regardless, it didn't at all feel like work, it was therapeutic bliss.

On a warm spring morning, I woke up to the loud sounds of my laptop overworking. The video had finally finished rendering, and it was ready to be uploaded. I remember that feeling of joy like it was yesterday. I wanted to create another one ASAP because I truly fell in love with the process! At this point, I couldn't remember the last time I left the house since I began editing the video. I needed to step out and get some fresh air. I went to the nearest diner and enjoyed a pancake two-egg special while reflecting on my achievement. I returned to my laptop on a full stomach and officially uploaded the video to the World Wide Web.

My friend and I put forth our best efforts to get the word out about the music video. When we shared it with people, the reactions were usually mixed. It ranged from, "What the fuck is this weird shit I'm watching??" to "This is the most amazing thing I've ever seen!" Whatever the reaction, everyone agreed they had never seen anything like it.

One evening, I saw a comment on the video that read, "I've just seen this on TV!" Now, I'm not exactly sure how it caught on, but it started buzzing. I watched the views go from 200 to 20,000 in a short period of time. It may not have been a lot to someone else, but I was excited. This one video seemed to be getting more attention than anything I've put out on the Internet. I immediately called my friend and said,

"Dude! Let's work on the next one!" I confidently told him, between us recording the songs on his dated equipment and me doing the video production, we can keep it all in-house and keep creating. He agreed without hesitation because at this time, he grew to love the process as well. So, we produced another music video and boom! Even more views! It was crazy to know my art was finally being seen, granted it was an unorthodox route, but it was still being seen. The videos seemed so unique people didn't know what to make of it at first glance, but I didn't care. Some people would say, "Is this serious? Is this guy some kind of joke?" But those comments didn't bother me; like I said, I enjoyed stimulating people's emotions, whatever kind of feeling it was.

There were many naysayers, but for every hater, there were seven admirers. There was a large community that did appreciate the art in its entirety, big enough for a sizable fan base to begin forming. Soon people began emailing us from all over the world expressing their love, cable television shows were asking to use our videos for segments and bloggers started requesting interviews. We were on a hot roll like microwaved pastrami and cheese from a New York deli.

As things progressively grew, we had people's attention. I knew this was the perfect time to put a team together; a movement consisting of like-minds. It was time to include the people I met on my journey, just as I vowed in the contract I created for myself a few years prior.

Involving friends in my projects has always been my forte, but this was really a legit opportunity to display all of our talents to the world, even if it's not the traditional route. I told my homie who was now my business partner the move I was about to make and he couldn't agree more. We were both cut from the same cloth when it came to being selfless.

For so long, I'd cross paths with artists who related to my story. People who were talented but may have been overlooked in their fields or simply just fed up with the industry cliques and politics. I knew so many talented artists from singers to producers, so putting together a collective made sense. I came up with the name *Turquoise Jeep Records* for the label; it symbolized unity, we ride for each other no matter the circumstances. The name was meant to be as abstract as the content we produced. It would be a platform where creative freedom would be limitless, and zero fucks would be given when making art.

The vision was manifesting; within two years of this idea, we amassed millions of views from several music videos that went viral like: *Fried or Fertilized, Cavities,* and *Lemme Smang It* to name a few. People I haven't heard from in years randomly began calling just to prove to people they knew me. "Aye, man! Tell my girlfriend that you and I are good friends! She doesn't believe me!" I would often hear. Apparently, calling me on speakerphone was a good way to get coochie points.

As the views grew, so did the fans. Our popularity kept spreading. Interviews, radio plays, people from all over were wearing Flynt Flossy shirts and creating fan videos. Kids nationwide began dressing as me for Halloween, I couldn't believe my eyes. Whether you considered us too popular to be labeled underground or not famous enough to be labeled mainstream, I knew we officially made our arrival in pop culture history.

The newfound fame was a blessing, but being famous wasn't what drove me. I loved developing as a versatile artist and growing with other like-minds. The more material we put out, the more people noticed our growth, even to the point other creatives were anxious to collaborate.

I loved being able to write a song hook for an artist, see how they would interpret it, shoot a visual, and watch it all take off. This lane gave me so much freedom, I'm having a ball! I was so thankful for this new platform where artists' talents can be recognized. So, whether I was behind the scenes filmmaking, music producing, writing or whatever, I just wanted to keep making shit. So, I kept cranking them out, and it kept spreading.

One music video in particular that really caught people's attention was entitled, *Did I mention I Like to Dance.* Up until this point, I held back from the public I had a career in dance. I remember my biz partner telling me during preproduction, "You need to dance your ass off in this video! It's time to show the world what you really can do!" So, I did dance my ass off, and he was absolutely right. It was after this video more people began taking us seriously as performers. The general reaction of most people seemed to be, "Holy shit! This dude can actually dance!"

The video gained over a million views faster than I could imagine. Soon after it went viral, we began getting offers to headline live concerts. Coincidentally, this was also around the same time a good friend of mine opened her own dance studio. So not only would we have a plush spot to rehearse, but she was also down to choreograph our live show, the timing was crazy. Everything seemed to be moving at such a fast pace, but it was all making sense, the stars were rapidly aligning.

One warm afternoon, six of us packed into an SUV en route to Indianapolis; it would be our first time headlining a live show. It was a road trip like no other. We talked, laughed, and jammed out to music anticipating what was ahead. As we pulled up to the venue for sound check, I said jokingly to my biz partner, "I hope people actually show up," and he agreed with my statement. As we all walked inside the venue, the promoter ran up to us and said, "Holy fuck! You guys are actually real! This as an honor! It's sold out tonight!" I thought he was putting on a cruel joke, so I laughed it off and whispered to myself, "Sold out? What a dick-cheese to toy with our emotions." But honestly, if only 12 people showed up, I would have been just as excited, I was just grateful for it all.

Later that night after a bite to eat and some rest at the hotel, we made our way back to the venue for Showtime. As we followed the promoter through a dark alley leading to backstage, I went over the choreography in my head feeling butterflies in my stomach. When we entered the backstage dressing room, I could hear crowd chatter by the door leading to the main stage. I grew curious, it sounded like way more than the 12 people I anticipated. So, I decided to peek my head out the cracked double doors, and to my surprise, the promoter wasn't joking! It was a packed house! Within a couple of seconds of my head being exposed, a group of eager women caught a glimpse of me and screamed, "OMG! IT'S FLYNT FLOSSY!" They began to rush towards the door screaming, almost knocking over security. I closed the doors in a panic and at that very moment, I realized...shit just got real.

We hit the stage to a roaring crowd that already knew the lyrics to every song. I was drenched with sweat as I pulled out every dance move in my arsenal. Suddenly, time slowed down in my head like a scene straight out of a Matrix movie. As I looked around the stage and saw my friends along with the adoring crowd, I was overwhelmed with a feeling of joy. People were enjoying themselves, and my friends were steps closer to their dreams all because of an idea I pursued. The contract I made to myself was materializing before my very eyes.

We ended our energetic set as the crowd chanted, "Encore! Encore!" Security escorted us from the side of the stage and led us through the rowdy adoring crowd. It felt like we were the Beatles, the way people were reacting to the sight of us. It was crazy to hear so many people ask for my autograph. I remember thinking, "Huh? Who, me? You want my autograph? Why?" To them, I was a rock star, but deep down inside I was still that weird kid from the Bronx trying to figure out his life.

After finally getting through the thick crowd, we made it to our SUV parked outside. All six of us jumped inside and sat in total silence for a full minute with looks of disbelief. Then, someone broke the silence shouting, "Floss! You're a motherfucking genius, bro!" I laughed it off; the moment wasn't about me. I saw myself as but a vessel the universe was speaking through, all this was meant to happen.

Word soon got out we were a must-see show, people said we gave off an energy unprecedented. Fans flew in from Australia to England just to get a glimpse. Our shows were selling out all over the country, and we would spend hours after every concert signing autographs and taking pictures with every fan in the building. Things would escalate from there: magazine articles, nationwide wide tours, TV production meetings at fancy restaurants, and all other types of opportunities.

With more notoriety came more attention from women. I've always been the charismatic type as I mentioned earlier, so affection from a woman wasn't new to me, but I must say this was a different level, whoa! I must have missed the memo, but apparently, we became sex symbols. So did all the new lady attention get to my head? Not at all, but I damn sure didn't mind being desired, I tell you that much. There were times where women would whisper in my ear, "I want your sexy moves in my bed so bad, a night with you is my fantasy" or even slip their hotel room key in my pocket and say, "Come see me tonight, babe. You don't have to knock." It was nuts and took a while to sink in. Always hearing stories of rock stars getting caught up by women with ulterior motives made me extremely cautious of who I kept in my company. I was careful not to catch every lace bra and panty set that was thrown in my face, if you get what I mean.

I thought back to my days of working at a call center when I overheard women chat amongst themselves by the water cooler and swoon over their favorite celebrity. They would say, "Mmm, yes, girl, if I get one night with that sweet piece of man meat, I'd eat him alive!" And oh shit, at this very moment, I'm that "sweet piece of man meat" they'd be referring to. I've now become some sort of fetish, and I totally didn't mind.

As I walked through crowds, women would grab for me at all angles, tug at my sweaty clothes, try to get anything they could call a memento; even if it was an imprint of my sweat on the side of their face. Hearing a woman beg to take home my dirty T-shirt as a souvenir after we just had sex wasn't something I was quite used to. "PLEASE let me have this! I just want a part of you to take home with me!" I would hear.

Were ladies an inspiration? I'd be lying like a cheap beaver skin rug if I said no, but that was just icing on the cake for me. You see, for years, I had created and been rejected; I worked so damn hard, and FINALLY, I was tasting some fruits of my labor. I'm not saying we were super celebrity millionaires or anything, but it was just crazy to see progress.

For the first time in forever, I felt a sense of relief. Was I at all complacent? Absolutely not; I'm the kind of person that gets motivated by progress, not comfortable. I knew there were so many more people who haven't heard of us yet. I had to have a different kind of work ethic being we were independent with little to no outside help.

However, I was guilty of thinking it would get easier from this point, and that definitely wasn't the case. There was so much that came with it all and the majority of the time, I wasn't prepared. Yes, I endured a whole lot on my journey; my road consisted of twists, turns, potholes, you name it. But I also received an abundance of blessings. I've met amazing people, experienced priceless moments, and till this day, I'm still able to do what I love with a lot more growth and learning ahead of me. They say the best way to build character is through experience. So whatever I went through, whether it was good or bad, contributed to my development, you feel me? So, I want you to gain from my experiences and philosophies in some form or fashion, let my thoughts on various topics stimulate your perspective and contribute to your journey.

3

Even True Heroes Can Be Viewed as
Villains in Someone Else's Story

It's an indescribable feeling to see your dreams transpire. It was so crazy to me, it's like everything I ever wanted was in the midst of manifesting. But as blissful as it seemed, the reality of the situation began sinking in. While there were many people happy about the newfound success, I began to notice something else. I would notice this weird negative energy consume some people around me and attitudes towards me began to alter. You can only imagine how new this was for me; my whole life, I was always "that cool guy that never bothered anyone." But I suddenly became a target, and this was a big culture shock. People's "random acts of kindness" would have hidden intentions: "Hey, man, remember that time I did that thing for you? Well, you owe me for that. You're an Internet celebrity, I know you got it!"

I began questioning myself on what the hell was going on. Is it something I'm doing that's making people act so different towards me? Am I the one that's changed? Am I giving off some kind of vibe unbeknownst to me? All I wanted was to pave a way, do something no one has ever done. But I would realize being a trailblazer had both its pros and cons

You see, we started seeing success on the internet at a time when it wasn't as saturated; a time when you told a friend, "Someone called me from YouTube" and their response would be, "Real people actually work at YouTube?" It was dope to be a pioneer, but being it was all relatively new, people's curiosity was at a high, and many questions began to arise. I would hear stuff like, "Hey, man, my friend's mom's cousin's mechanic told me that people get $1 per view on the internet. So, since you have millions of views, I know you're close to half a billion dollars in your bank account, right?"

When I heard statements like that, I wondered, *What in the hell are some of these people talking about? And why do they all of a sudden want to pull out their abacus and act like they have a mathematical degree from an Ivy League school?!*

I was under constant scrutiny, I felt like my every word and action was being examined under a microscope. People's eyes were on me like pee stains on a public urinal. Whenever I would speak, *I wasn't telling enough* and when I didn't say much, *I was keeping secrets.* It seemed as if they were waiting for me to slip up in some way so they can say, "AH HA! I gotcha! I knew you were up to something!" The smallest thing, from me wearing a new shirt, would cause people to overanalyze and raise suspicion of me secretly having stacks of cash stuffed under my mattress. I was stuck in a strange "damned if you do and damned if you don't" alternate universe because of my newfound success, and I was so confused.

One day, I randomly asked my friend and business partner if he felt the same way I did about people around him, and he responded, "Hell yea, I noticed something! People are acting crazy, bro, and I don't understand why."

Reality eventually settled in, and I realized what actually changed was people's perception of me, some for the good and some for the bad. There were people that began viewing me as some sort of product with the potential of being a meal ticket. Some became less sincere because to them it was now a game of chess; they became cold and calculated. I felt like some people were solely around me to be in a position to reap benefits, in case I got "face on the front of soda cans and super bowl commercials" famous. And, know this, there is a big difference between someone who genuinely believes in your vision and wants to see it grow and someone who just doesn't want to miss out on an opportunity. You have to be cognizant of that.

While I celebrated being bestowed this new platform, others were acting on assumptions and counting imaginary dollars that haven't yet been acquired. What the fuzzy fuck? Have I entered *The Twilight Zone* or something? People started coming at my neck from left and right for minuscule things.

I remember being at a sushi restaurant and venting to both my biz partner and my lawyer, friends I confided in. My lawyer, who was such a savior throughout many of my rough times, put down his bowl of steaming miso soup and said with the sincerest face, "I've been doing this job a long time and this is by far some of the craziest shit I've heard. It's like you're seen as a golden cow and everyone is trying to stake their claim. You're a good guy, Floss; I'm sorry you have to go through all this."

It all became so overwhelming I sunk into a sad space. And on top of it all, my dad, the man I always saw as my superhero, began undergoing cancer treatment. I kept it to myself because everyone seemed so caught up in their own wants that I doubt they would've been sympathetic; they must have missed the memo about me being a human being with emotions. But either way, I wasn't searching for sympathy, that's not my style. So, I just concealed my pain and suited up my spiritual armor.

I grew more worried at every fancy dinner with a TV producer that promised me a better life. You see, I was secretly afraid of becoming more famous. I would ask myself, "If people are acting like this towards me now, what the hell is going to happen if I get even bigger?" At a point, I felt like maybe it was better when people viewed this whole vision as some weird, stupid idea with no potential, rather than something on the verge of making millions; that way I wouldn't have been exposed to people's greed. I came into this with the purest intentions, but I would basically become a faceless entity that was a source of income. The narrative for some seemed to be, "Let's get what we can out this guy while it lasts." It was a rude awakening.

I didn't have the easiest life growing up, so I was conditioned to have tough skin. But I think the reason why I was so disappointed by some people's ugly behavior was because it was unwarranted and unexpected. Of course, you hear all the crazy stories in those celebrity documentaries on TV, but you don't know how true it is until it actually happens to you.

One morning, while sipping my strawberry-banana and kale smoothie, I thought to myself, *Why am I afraid of elevating? Am I really that worried about how others will view me? Man, I'm straight buggin' right now!* Yea, I was going through a lot of bullshit, but there was plenty of good that came with the bad. I created a livelihood from an idea. Not only was I doing what I loved, but I also had a dedicated fan base that appreciated it. I couldn't allow any negativity to steal my joy, plus there were still people in my corner who knew my intentions were pure.

Yeah, it was all new to me, but I had to figure it out and adapt; it took a lot of meditating and reflecting, but I eventually threw cold water on my face and got my shit together. I couldn't let my emotions run me. So as my 3rd grade teacher used to tell us, I put on my big boy pants and tied on my thinking cap. I put things into perspective objectively and analyzed the matter at hand.

Now that my mind was clearer, I was able to really think, hmm...I truly didn't believe everyone coming at my neck were evil at the core. So, what would make someone act ugly even when I give my best efforts? The brutally honest friends in my life that didn't alter through it all reassured me I hadn't changed one bit. I was still the same cool Flynt Flossy in their eyes. So, with that being said, I wanted to tackle the root of some people's nasty behavior; what's making them trip over cordless phones? As in paranoid for no damn reason.

Ok, so check it out, this was what I assessed: When you attain success, some people will begin to expect things from you. So, the issues some people may have won't be about the things you're doing TO them, but, actually, the things they feel you're NOT doing FOR them. This will cause people to perceive you differently without you even being aware. Mentally accept that you can't please everyone, and if you constantly try, you are susceptible to losing yourself in the process. I know that sounds generic, but trust me, you won't truly understand the depth of that statement until you are actually in the position, and it affects you most if you're the people-pleaser type.

Sometimes no matter how good your intentions are, you will still be viewed as the bad guy, to some. You can have all the traits of a true hero, but be seen as a villain in someone else's story. But that doesn't at all mean you're a bad person. Some people just view you differently at this time, and that's out of your control. They just don't react well to not getting their way. In these instances ask yourself,

"Was I fair to this person who has issues with me?" and "Did I give it my all?" If the answers are YES, then all you can really do is keep moving forward, feel me?

If someone is truly down for you, whatever disappointment they have will be temporary, because they know ultimately your intentions are pure. So, stay spiritually grounded and know as long as you do right by people and give it your all, you can be good with yourself, whatever the outcome. I feel it's very important to be at peace with what you see in the mirror.

4

Understanding Who's Aboard Your Vision Plane

So, check it out, you've reached an emboldened mental state, you got your mind right, ready to put that foot forward towards your dreams. This is probably when you are most vulnerable especially during the earlier stages of your journey. Hence, it's important you're aware of the kinds of people that will be in and out your life. Understand their roles on your journey. Personally, it took me going through rough times to realize everyone in my life weren't on the same page as I presumed.

Compare you pursuing your dreams to an airplane and you're the captain, destined to soar to new heights. You are the pilot of your "vision plane" and will have different kinds of passengers.

Some will be like-minded and share your vision. These are the type of people whose energy alone will inspire you to elevate. They will be passionate, encouraging, and won't allow you to quit in times of self-doubt. They see the bigger picture and ultimately desire the same thing. They will be understanding if turbulence occurs out of your control and even help think of solutions because, essentially, they are in it for the long haul. When you cross paths with these kinds of connections, sincerely appreciate them because they don't come along every day.

Some passengers will just be along for the ride. The type of people that will show up to pop champagne and eat cake in times of celebration, but will be the first to strap on their parachute and abandon you in times of adversity. Are they praying for your downfall? Not necessarily, they're not concerned if you win or lose. They strategically attach themselves to the situation because whatever you're doing at the moment is working and they're solely concerned with ways they can benefit.

Then there will also be passengers whose energy can be so outwardly negative it's toxic. When there is any kind of turbulence, their finger will always point at you. They become agitated at minuscule things because, essentially, they rather be somewhere else. The negativity they exude will make it uncomfortable for the people aboard your flight, sometimes even influencing the impressionable. In extreme cases, they secretly may not want your dream to manifest. I know it sounds crazy, but it definitely happens.

Whatever personalities you come across in the spectrum, be aware that whatever feels like dead weight can only weigh your vision plane down from soaring to new heights. People will usually reveal their true self in times of adversity, and it will be your choice to continue dealing with them or not. You heard that saying, "When people show you who they are, believe them"? Well, it's very true. I often found myself ignoring signs and trying to cater to passengers on my vision plane, I felt hardly contributed or even seemed toxic. Take it from me, it can come back to bite you in the ass!

I was in awe of some people's reactions when my vision plane had turbulence. It seemed all good when things were running smooth, but the minute some nutty dude pops up threatening legal action, because he feels you owe him money for borrowing his crayons in kindergarten, backs would turn fast as hell. During my rough times, I've witnessed people around me suddenly stop using the words WE and US, and began saying YOU and Y'ALL.

Situations like this can be disheartening at first, but don't let it break you. This shouldn't dim your light nor slow you down. It's just the universe's way of revealing what you needed to see, clearing paths for your true blessings to come. It's all gravy, stay your course, and the right passengers will organically be placed in your plane when the time calls for it.

5

The Importance of Holding Yourself Accountable, but Not Enabling Entitlement

Pride and ego can be a person's downfall. It takes a certain level of maturity to acknowledge your faults and an even higher level to apologize for them. If you always feel you're the victim and lack the ability to be introspective, you can never truly grow as a person. So, I applaud you if you are the type to hold yourself accountable when you are at fault. However, I also say this, be very careful not to enable people's sense of entitlement. Because once you set that tone, it can come back to smack you in the face.

There was a point in time where I found myself always unnecessarily apologizing to people, instead of holding them accountable for their actions. I would say sorry just because I felt the word would fix things. This dream I worked so hard for was finally becoming a reality, so the last thing I wanted was for someone around me to be unhappy. I just wanted to keep going, keep creating, as there was so much more to achieve, and I needed everything to run smooth. But while I thought saying sorry would fix things, even at times I felt I wasn't in the wrong, it actually made shit worse.

It's almost as if my unnecessary apologies set the tone for people to believe they were always right and I was always in the wrong; I eventually began to sense an energy of entitlement develop. You know what? Maybe I can't completely fault people; I mean if someone were always telling you sorry, how else would you feel? But I figured it was a way to keep consistent peace around me. Look, maybe it's the Libra in me, but I hate conflict and try to avoid it. I just wanted to create without confrontation. Unfortunately, when you take that approach, people can begin to always expect from you, even with little to no contribution. They may not even mean harm, but because you enabled their entitlement, it's what's they grew used to.

I remember one particular time, someone who was close to me asked to borrow some money. Well, actually, it was more than "some," it was a whole damn lot. This wasn't the first time either; I lent him money on several occasions, even if it hurt my pockets. But this time I just wasn't in the position to do it again, especially the amount he asked for. When I told him I couldn't do it, he got angry and called me disloyal, because in his own mind, I was "holding out." I said yes a million times before, but the one time I said no because I just didn't have it, all the times I said yes didn't matter. And the crazy thing, I actually felt guilty for a second. Him saying I didn't have his back made me feel bad. But at the same time, a part of me was also infuriated. I wanted to put my knuckles to his cheekbone, straight Rocky Balboa style. I just couldn't believe he used the word "disloyal."

Throughout my career, whether it was dance, film, music, or whatever, I've always configured ways to include people close to me. And not because I had some sort of ulterior motive, but because I had the best intentions of creating paths everyone could benefit from. I wanted us all to win together, feel me? I had a deep value for the concept of unity and loyalty.

I would often put people before myself. There were plenty of times I gave someone my last dime knowing I had other responsibilities. Even when it came to music, I would write a hot song and take the backseat to another artist. I knew they would receive all the credit, but I'd rather play the background and see them elevate. And I say all this not expecting praises because I always viewed being appreciative as a two-way street. I say all this to simply paint a picture. I want you to understand my emotions, how it felt to hear the word "disloyal" from someone you sacrificed so much for. He seemed so spoiled by me always giving in, and it felt very one-sided.

One night, I had an epiphany hit me harder than stale cheesy bread. Why the hell did I initially feel guilty saying, "I can't?" I began to realize I was always telling people "sorry, I couldn't GIVE you this" or "my bad, I wasn't able to GIVE you that." When I think back to it, all those unnecessary apologies set an entitled tone.

Now, am I saying I was always perfect in every dispute that transpired? Nah, only a fool would say they're perfect. I'm a firm believer in holding yourself accountable if you're at fault, even if your actions meant no harm. But I can confidently say, I didn't deserve the inconsiderate responses from some people around me. I was always overextending, trying to make everyone happy, cheating myself in the process. And as I stated earlier, that's an easy way to wear yourself out and often for people that won't even appreciate your efforts. Remember, all you can do is your best and be as fair as possible.

Ok, here is a quick exercise. I want you to take a second and reflect... did a valuable relationship you have go bad? What was the reason? Were you at fault? Is it worth fixing? If so, I challenge you to call that person and make amends. A valuable relationship is not worth losing over a mere disagreement, which can be resolved with one phone call. In the same token, be cognizant of people who constantly feel they are the victim because unbeknownst to them they can become the victimizer. If you are the only one always holding yourself accountable, it can end up being one-sided, which is a toxic relationship.

So hear me on this, no matter how significant someone's role is when it comes to your bigger picture, don't be afraid to call them out on their bullshit rather than saying "sorry" just to pacify. If that person is true, they will respect your stance. You all should be able to hash it out and eventually go back to being cool. You're not always wrong just like they're not always right. If you find yourself always being the mature one in the matter, then it's probably a relationship not worth having anyway.

I found myself always saying sorry without reciprocity. Remember, I grew up in the hood, so I'm not some docile chump you can just walk over, but my dreams made me vulnerable and unfortunately, some people would use that against me. I took shit I wouldn't have usually taken from people, because I knew how vital it was to hold my composure. At a point, the narrative became "you can get what you want out of Flossy. He'll always fold because this is 'his thing' and he just wants to keep it going." I exacerbated the tone of entitlement unbeknownst to me. And like I said, pride and ego are toxic, but self-respect is essential, especially to remain strong enough to keep your dream thriving.

6

*Forcing Someone to Share Your Vision
Cheats Everyone Involved*

As a visionary, sometimes we can get so caught up in the bigger picture, we're blinded from our surroundings. But the fact you have tunnel vision doesn't mean it's ok to immerse yourself in negativity. Negative energy you're surrounded with can take you off track. Not only is it unhealthy for your spirit, but it's also not conducive to your greater goal.

Not everyone needs to believe in your vision, and it's not your job to break your neck trying to convince them either. You must have value in your dream.

Say for instance, you were in a marriage, would you want to have to force your partner to love you unconditionally? I'm guessing a majority of you would say no. Well, it's kind of like the same thing, feel me? Think about it, when you make someone a part of your vision, you form a relationship. Like any relationship, you will go through ups and downs; not everyone will be in it for the long haul, and that's okay. Some people may lose interest in your vision over time, while others may have seen it as a cool opportunity for the time being, but never had a genuine care for it.

However, if someone just isn't interested in your vision that doesn't necessarily make them a bad person. Are you at fault for favoring butter pecan over fudge ripple? No, everyone is entitled to how they feel and you can't knock them for that. So, no matter how bad you want to involve someone in your vision, you have to learn to be ok with letting go. Now, what you can analyze is how that person handled the situation.

Ask yourself, was he or she upfront about their disinterest, but you forced their involvement anyway? Or were they deceitful and made you think otherwise because they were opportunistic? These are questions you have to ask yourself before you go pointing blame saying, "Woe is me."

I often found myself putting up with negativity in my environment because I was so focused on the greater goal. I've endured comments from people on my vision plane like:

"Floss, you're a novelty act, and you won't last
more than two years."

"Fuck the fame, fuck the fans, I'm ONLY here
for the money!"

"I could be doing other things. This is holding
me back from better opportunities!"

"Yeah, I know I'm being selfish, but so what.
You have to be selfish in this business!"

The list of unfavorable comments goes on.

I remember one time we got word that a Grammy-winning producer was a big fan of mine and wanted to work with me. I was honored and humbled when I received the news. But, unfortunately, my bubble was immediately popped by mood-killing remarks from someone on my end. "That dude has to be lying about having Grammy! Anyone who wants to work with YOU can't possibly be legit," he said aloud.

I often thought to myself, *Well, damn...did I really just hear someone say that? Aren't we supposed to be on the same team? What the fuck? Do they know I'm sitting right here?* It's almost as if strangers believed in me more than some people who were a part of my vision. People I would meet for the first time encouraged me to always keep going, while those who were close made discouraging comments like, "You can't possibly be serious about all of this. You actually think this 'little thing' will last much longer???" It was crazy to know there were people on my vision plane so ready to count me out and abandon me when the chips were down. But I was always able to stay focused and shrug off their negativity.

To be completely objective, they may've not even realized how gloomy their comments were to me, and they were just expressing how they honestly felt. But even though I was mentally strong enough to endure it, I still shouldn't have chosen to deal with it.

When people around you emit that type of dispiriting energy, it can subtly impact your thought process. At vulnerable moments in my life, I found myself thinking aloud, *"Damn, maybe they were right? Maybe my 'cute little run,' as they defined it, was over and I should give up as they said."* But hell nah, they weren't right at all, and your dreams are much too valuable to ever be compromised.

In hindsight, I should've distanced myself from certain people early on, but I looked past their uncomplimentary ways because I was so focused on including them in the bigger picture I envisioned, even if I sensed their disinterest. But that way of thinking only makes things worse, and people can grow comfortable being shitty towards you because, essentially, they could care less and rather be somewhere else. Your persistence to keep them around may translate in their head as, "you NEEDING them" in order to move forward. And unfortunately, some people will abuse the leverage they feel they have over you.

You have to come to terms with the fact that everyone won't see what you see and that's perfectly fine. So, if you part ways with someone, don't be bitter or wish them bad. Be grateful for whatever goals you have achieved together or just be grateful you didn't get farther than you needed to with them. Because, at the end of the day, when you force someone to share your vision, you're cheating yourself, them, and the bigger picture. Letting go can be bittersweet if it's not what you foresaw, but trust me, it's a lame ass feeling being around someone who wants to be somewhere else.

I found myself missing out on great business opportunities because someone on my end intentionally ignored my phone calls. I also found myself chasing individuals to do paid gigs I had already lined up, I couldn't figure it out? I have to chase you, to pay you? It didn't make sense to me? Well, maybe feeling "needed" stroked some people's ego, who knows. But whatever the reason, I was devaluing my dream. I'm guilty of being loyal to a fault at times, which is why I kept making attempts, but once I learned to let go and let be, great things started to happen. New opportunities presented themselves, and so many amazing people would begin entering my life, it was like clockwork. I began to feel so much better about myself. All the positivity I began to attract was reassurance that I was in the right direction. It was so refreshing to cross paths with humble like-minded people on the same spiritual frequency as me. *Whoa! These people are actually appreciative of the efforts I put forth? This is crazy, I've been missing out on so much all this time!* It's been a while since I experienced some reciprocity. I told myself never again would I focus on those who didn't care to be included because it distracts you from people who would kill for such an opportunity.

Appreciate what you learn from your experiences so you can take your lessons to the next phase of your journey. Don't ever cheat yourself by forcing someone to share your vision, have value in your dreams, and know there are people out there that want to share and support your vision. So, it's unhealthy to settle with someone who doesn't.

7

Outside Opinions Can Have the Best
Intentions, but Do the Worst Damage

I believe the famous saying is, "Opinions are like assholes, everybody has one." Well, I'll take it one step further; a lot of them can stink too. I've learned when your business is out in the open, you become susceptible to corruptive outside views. One thing you'll learn if you haven't already is, everybody always has something to say. Someone always wants to tell you what you should or should not be doing, and what he or she would do in your shoes. The opinions of others can mean well, but do the most harm, especially if that person or persons giving the advice have no kind of experience in your situation. So that random bearded dude at the coffee shop that happened to overhear your escalating phone conversation might not have the best advice for you to follow verbatim.

I've seen plenty of situations go left because someone followed some random inaccurate advice. I'm not saying you shouldn't hear out different constructive perspectives from people who care about you, because that's perfectly cool. As humans, it's therapeutic to have someone to vent to, it keeps us balanced. At the same time, just be real selective about who you let know your personal business. Everyone may not have your best interest at heart.

I'll be the first to tell you, I have a handful of close friends and family that I often get advice from. Even though they are always 100% honest; at the end of the day, it's still up to me to use my best judgment before taking action. Even when friends ask me for advice, I always give a disclaimer, "This is just my insight, take what you feel applies best."

Yes, your loved ones want what's best for you. However, if you tell them about a disagreement you had with someone, and their response is "You need to call them right now and show 'em who's boss!" that doesn't necessarily mean it's the next move you should immediately make. Only you know the true details of your situation. So, while people mean well, there will be some natural bias because they only hear your side.

Believe it or not, everyone you have a falling out with may not have the ill intent you think. I know, that concept was hard for me to digest at first, but it's true. When you're on bad terms with a person, it's hard not to view them in a negative light. But in retrospect, I noticed whenever someone had an issue with me, the first thing they would say usually began with "hey, someone told me..." as if they were influenced. I would get approached with the wildest theories from some people. I almost wanted to laugh in their face because they were so confident in their outlandish assumptions. I would just think, *Huh? Where the hell are you getting your information from, bruh? Let me know so I can never go there because you're straight pissing out your mouth right now.*

But viewing it all objectively helped me understand why some people's attitudes towards me would suddenly switch up like day and night. In a nutshell, I feel people from the outside looking in, put some bullshit in their ear. They were just impressionable and fell victim to the opinions of those who were probably not experienced in the matter.

You remember growing up, how most playground fights started because of instigators and spectators from the sideline? You know, that one kid that would whisper in your ear, "I wouldn't take that if I were you!" In the hood, we call this "putting the bug in your ear" or "the battery in your back." Next thing you know, issues arise because of foolish pride, and you start creating false notions that are far from the truth.

So, if some venting to a friend or family member helps emotionally, then, by all means, do it. I know it helps me. I talk my big brother's ear off all the time, but I still have a mind of my own, and that's very important. When you live by everyone else's opinions, you can lose your true self. You can become a puppet to other people's thoughts, making decisions you may not even truly believe in, but you were just convinced by someone else. Remember, at the end of the day, you're the one dealing with the consequences of your actions.

So, check it out, before you follow through with someone's advice, ask yourself:

- Does this person I'm confiding in have experience on this topic?
- Am I looking for direction or just venting?
- Was I fair in telling all sides of the story?

Take bits and pieces from the people you respect, formulate your own assessment, and apply it to your situation. I've witnessed some good relationships crumble because someone who didn't do their own research decided to take the crappy advice of a third cousin's sister's dentist who really didn't know shit.

8

Don't Let the Relationships that Fold Force You to Travel a Lonely Road

You may encounter disappointments on your journey; people you feel let you down with broken promises and false commitments. You begin to feel betrayed and have a moment where you say to yourself, "Why did I let them get that close? From now on I don't need anyone but myself!" Moving forward, it's important not to let these bad experiences consume you, perpetually tarnishing your spirit and permanently making you a bitter person, unwilling to let anyone get close. Yea, I know it's easier said than done, but reflect for a second...do you really want to do EVERYTHING all alone?

Don't get me wrong, it's important to be well-versed at all positions in your field. For instance, if you're a small business owner establishing a restaurant, you want to be knowledgeable about running the cash register, hopping on the grill, bussing tables, and handing out your marketing flyers if need be; whatever you need to do to prepare for the worst-case scenarios. However, I wouldn't suggest taking on all those rolls to be your main objective. Yeah, it may be possible, but you'll burn yourself out.

Trust me, I get it. Sometimes you're left no choice when you can't find help. In my earlier filming days, there were times I put my camera on a tripod, pressed record, and ran back into the frame. I kept repeating the process until I got it right. So yeah, I got it done, but talk about exhausting! I yearned for a little help; that way I could focus on the major things instead of spreading myself thin with the minor things, having a team gives optimal results.

Throughout my journey, I can say I've had my fair share of disappointments by people. There were several occasions I invested my time, efforts, and money into a person, only to be let down for whatever reason. In other words, roll the dice on someone and crap out. During my upset moments, some friends I confided in would advise me to stop having such a big heart and looking out for other people. "Floss, you need to start doing EVERYTHING solo," I would hear. I knew they meant well with their words, but that just wasn't my style, you feel me? "Drain yourself clenching the spotlight or grow by sharing the stage," is my philosophy.

Think about your favorite celebrity, whether it's an actor, musician, or whoever. They all have a strong team behind them, no matter how solo they appear. Do you really think they're doing it all by themselves? That would be pretty rare and if they are, good chance they have high blood pressure from all the stress.

I'm just saying, don't aim to wear all the hats because of inner issues you developed. Remind yourself that everyone isn't identical. Let your judgment of a person be strictly based on that individual's own actions. You'll often hear people say, "Trust absolutely NO ONE." But personally, I always took that phrase with a grain of salt. Balance is very important to me. I don't want to become that bitter dude who can't move on, that guy who is always mad at the world and on edge 24/7 because in his mind, "everybody is the EXACT SAME!" I think that's a wack way to live. Maybe it's just me, but I feel at least some level of trust is needed in order to elevate, not for EVERYONE of course. I'm not saying walk around like a naïve gullible doofus, because you definitely have to be on your toes for sketchy people. But it's also vital that you balance your spirit.

People disappointing you is just a part of the process, view your past bad experiences as learning lessons to grow from. Now you know how to maneuver the next go-round. You know what steps to take to prevent bad situations from reoccurring or how to bounce back faster if they do. My approach is more like this: "Everyone I let into my life starts on a clean slate, but if their actions show they can't be 100% trusted, then I'll know how to act accordingly." Everyone has their own methods, this is just mine.

A lack of trust is usually what makes people want to do everything by themselves. But when you keep expecting people to do you wrong, you can become a prisoner of your own thoughts, creating false narratives in your head. If you keep instilling in your mind "something bad will happen," you can mentally psyche yourself out. Even focusing on what you can find negative in someone's kind gesture, your extreme paranoia can stifle your potential growth by sabotaging good situations; it's just not the healthiest of ways to function if you ask me. Don't take for granted how special it is when you find people with good chemistry and are on your same mental frequency. Don't chase them away because you are jaded from bad past experiences.

9

*Whenever You're Weak at Heart, Think Back
to What Fueled Your Start*

Every so often, life can seem so overwhelming the
vision of your goals can be skewed. As human beings, we're
all susceptible to it. There were times I felt my style of art
was so unique it was preventing me from getting where I
wanted to be. It became discouraging always getting so close
to a life-altering opportunity and for some odd reason, it
falls through. Getting constantly rejected throughout my life
always forced me to create my own situations. I couldn't
book as a dancer, so I put together my own traveling dance

showcases. I couldn't get into traditional film festivals, so I created a platform for people to both see my visuals and hear my music. People would tell me I was diversely talented, but would rarely publicly cosign and then use my works without giving credit. I grew tired of being misunderstood. It got exhausting being too different to be digested by the masses.

Even at my current level, I can sometimes feel underrated and overlooked. Contrary to what some people believe, just because I took an unorthodox approach with my style of art doesn't make me any less of a "legit artist." The fact that there are still people keeping their admiration for my work private because they're concerned of what others may think can be frustrating. It's not until they meet another supporter they feel at ease. "Oh snap, you're a Flynt Flossy fan too?! Phew! I thought I was the only one!" I would often ask myself, "Why don't more people embrace liking something different rather than being embarrassed until they get approval from others?"

There were also times when people around me were so busy pushing their own agenda; they didn't realize how selfish and inconsiderate they were towards me. It all got so overwhelming at a point I had thoughts of saying "fuck it" and calling it quits.

You see, we all have our moments, but let them be just that, "a moment." Don't live in these bleak thoughts because they couldn't be farther from the truth. There is so much more left for you to do. There are so many people who believe and are counting on you.

I have this saying, "Whenever you're weak at heart, think back to what fueled your start." In times of doubt, think back to what gave you that first spark to chase your goals. I want you to take a second right now and reflect... Why did you start your journey? Now think of the reason why you made it this far. I'll tell you, it's because your initial intentions were pure. The early stages are always the most innocent; think back to what first gave you that fire. Think back to what kept you up all night because you couldn't stop envisioning it.

It's important to stay inspired, you feel me? Say if you're a discouraged dancer like I was at a point, take a class where you know you won't see any familiar faces. So, it won't be a matter of impressing "Gossip Gabby" because you know she'll be in attendance, and she's cool with all the top-booking agents. Take a second and say, "Fuck chasing people's approval." Forget about the politics, let it be strictly about passion. Better yet, pull out that full mirror from your bedroom closet, turn on some music and dance till you're drenched in sweat. This concept of revisiting your inspiration can be applied to anyone in any field. It can be as simple as looking at your children or reading the first poem you ever wrote, anything to remind you why you worked so hard in the first place.

Whenever I became uncertain of myself, I would remember that fan who emailed me saying my art got them through their depression or that fan who told me they spent the last of what they had to buy a ticket to my concert. I also thought about that joy I felt creating music with my friends and the excitement I'd get when I discovered a new video editing technique. These thoughts made me snap out of my stupor, I reassured myself and said, "Floss, you straight trippin' right now, dude! Look how far you've come. Look at the number of lives you touched and how many people love and support you."

So yea, I've been rejected more times than defective airbags on an assembly line; rejected to the point I just grew used to it, but maybe I'm just not meant to be normal. Maybe my unique form was never meant to fit in the traditional mold, but I can't dwell on it and see it as a disadvantage. It's okay to be different. Yea, it's a lot of extra work, but I know what I love to do and that keeps me inspired.

I want you to reflect whenever you have moments of uncertainty. I want you to know that you have a greater purpose and don't ever lose sight of that.

10

Stop. Chill. Breathe. Rationale Wins Races

Pursuing a vision can be an emotional rollercoaster, so it's vital to have a seatbelt of rationale. There will be some days you feel inspired, ready to conquer the world, and other days you feel down, questioning your life choices, we're all guilty of it. So, being our inner thoughts can be so unbalanced at times, we must be level-headed with our actions. Yeah, we can't control what goes on in our head sometimes, but we do have control of whether we act on those thoughts or not.

Our emotions can make us act out of character especially when it deals with what we're passionate about. So, before you send that lengthy angry email or make that enraged phone call to that individual that rubbed you the wrong way, stop, chill, and breathe. Think about it and ask yourself, "Are the potential consequences really worth it?" Because once you put it out into the universe, sometimes there is no going back. A moment of impulsivity can leave lifetime scars, create irreparable relationships, and ruin future opportunities. Not everyone will give you the pass for acting an ass. I've seen many people crash and burn driving an ego truck with a full tank of pride.

There were times when my cool and calm temperament was tested. The leadership position I was in made me an easy target for people's everyday frustrations in life. If someone had a bad day at home, blame it on Flossy. If someone's money was low, blame it on Flossy. If it rained outside when the forecast said clear skies all week, blame it on Flossy. It's as if I was viewed as a scapegoat and my kindness was taken for weakness.

On one or two occasions, my homie had to calm me down and hold me back from getting physical with a dude. I didn't care if I won or lost the fight, but I sure as hell would have gone out swinging. It's rare that I lose my cool, but I was tired of some people thinking it was okay to attack my character over what they theorized in their mind or be disrespectful because they had leverage, and knew my dream was at stake. As I said earlier, I never tried to be a gangster, but I'm no doormat either, don't get it twisted. You're not going to talk at me in any kind of way without me standing up for myself. But as I matured as an entrepreneur and as a person in general, I learned I couldn't handle situations like I once did growing up in the streets of New York. To lose your cool is a sign of how much control that person has over your emotions. I mean let's be real, no one is perfect, we all can fall victim to the heat of the moment. But just don't let anger consuming you be a routine, you feel me?

Our minds can play tricks on us; emotions can lead us to act on false notions created by our imagination. That being said, it's not wise to vilify people off of what you speculate in your own head without any definitive proof of them doing wrong.

So, remember to stop, chill, and breathe before you lose your cool or act on assumptions. Be rationale and don't let your feelings get the best of you. Get it in control and think level-headed before potentially convicting someone who may actually be innocent. Doing that can cost you more than you think and leave you with regrets later. Nothing is worse than being at fault for losing someone in your life that actually had your best interest at heart.

11

Value People Who Won't Sacrifice the Truth for the Sake of Being Strategic

We all strive to climb life's ladder, let's be real; it's humanistic to want to get ahead. However, be cognizant of the levels to this way of thinking, you feel me? When you become a person that constantly obsesses with getting ahead, you are susceptible to becoming shallow and opportunistic, and lose sight of what keeps you spiritually balanced.

I knew of individuals who purposefully disassociated themselves from genuine people in their lives because they felt "the relationship wouldn't benefit their career." They would say, "Why would I associate with someone if they can't do anything for me?" This mentality eventually led them feeling empty because there was a lack of authenticity around them. Being surrounded by people who could care less about you, until the next financial transaction can be depressing. It's all about balance, don't take genuine people in your life for granted, the people who will keep it real with you and don't always play chess.

We're all guilty of getting so caught up in our careers and chasing our goals, we can forget about the things that really matter in life. Like someone calling to simply say, "how are you?" with genuine concern. I still have childhood friends I'm close to that have nothing to do with my industry; they're authentic and have always been real with me. They'll buy tickets and come support my concerts because they're genuinely happy for my progress. They're proud I followed through with my passion, and I truly appreciate them. How could you not have a deep value for people like that? They're supportive with or without my notoriety.

When referring to a person in your life who gives you a false sense of reality, you'll hear people use the term "yes-men." But I think it goes deeper, you'll also come across people I refer to as "chess-men." I'll break it down, yes-men simply agree with you regardless of the circumstances in order to earn your approval. While chess-men solely concentrate on being strategic for their own personal gain. They do anything necessary to manipulate the narrative in order to get the outcome they desire. For example, say you're at odds with a rival, a chess-man will often "ride the fence" and play both sides. In your face, they will agree with all your views. But behind your back to your adversary, they'll change up and DISAGREE with all your views.

Now, it's totally normal to plan out your moves, especially if you're a wise businessperson, all good. But what makes chess-men different in my opinion is he or she wouldn't care about mutual benefaction. They are more likely to be selfish with their intentions and could give a shit about your best interest. They play a game and do anything necessary to come out the victor, even if takes being dishonest. There are levels to it, you feel me?

But however you look at it, you can't grow if the people around you constantly give you a false sense of reality, by telling you whatever they feel you want to hear. Yeah, I know it can be anybody. It's difficult figuring out which person is just feeding your ego, but it's way easier to determine the people who aren't. Because the ones who are not "gassing you up" won't be afraid to tell you when they disagree. However, people can sometimes misconstrue a friend having contrasting views with "hating," even if they are tactful in their approach. It's important to surround yourself with people that will uplift you and are truthful in the same light, in order to bring out your best.

For example, say you ask a friend to take a look at a project you're working on. They give you the honest critique you asked for. They tell you what they like and what they feel you can improve on. It may have not been exactly what you wanted to hear, but it doesn't at all mean they're hating on you. Maybe their truth is what you needed to hear in order to bring out your best. It's always up to you to either apply their suggestions or not. On the other hand, if their response lacked constructive ideas on how to improve and sounded more like, "Give up, it won't ever happen for you. I don't know why you even try," now, that sounds more like a hater, you get me?

I can say there were plenty of times a song or video I created came out better on my second attempt because I wasn't too prideful to hear a real friend's constructive criticism. There was one particular artist I worked with that was extremely sensitive. No one in the recording studio liked being honest with him because they didn't want to hurt his feelings. The most minor critiques made him defensive, no matter how nice you presented it. I often butted heads with him creatively because he felt I just wanted things my way. "You're always the only one saying something. Everyone else likes what I wrote!" he would say. But little did he know, I wasn't the only one who felt he should re-write his verse or didn't like a song idea of his, I was just the one to say it to his face. But, unfortunately, he often misconstrued my honesty and labeled me "a hater." I thought that notion was so damn ridiculous. Like really, are you kidding me? I just couldn't help being honest. I wanted the best for him and felt he had so much potential, but people holding back the truth was preventing him from reaching his true greatness.

There were times I felt submerged in a bogus self - preservative environment, where I'd hear people constantly talk bad about each other, and wouldn't be upfront for the sake of being in someone's good graces. Even when I spoke up and suggested that they take a more direct and truthful approach with the people they had issues with, in other words, say to their face and not behind their back, the reason they refused seemed more selfish and beneficial to themselves. It makes me cringe to be around someone who makes a habit of talking shit behind a person's back but smile in their face.

I always try to be as honest as I can with people. I'm not at all perfect, but I just try to be the best version of myself. Maybe that's why so many people confide in me?

They probably sense authenticity. Friends have even told me at times they were hesitant to ask for my insight because I was so real. "I knew I had to call you, but I wasn't quite ready for the truth," they would say. But I'm ok with that, you want someone who cares and sees the best in you, rather than someone with ulterior motives that says whatever to deceive you. Value those who won't sacrifice the truth, for the sake of being strategic. Because those are the ones who sincerely want to see you elevate, cherish it.

12

The Energy of Your Success May Uncover
Another Person's Insecurities

I'll start off by saying I'm a strong believer in energy. It's invisible and intangible, but definitely exists, if you ask me. You ever felt the presence of someone in a room without them saying a word, and were compelled to approach them? Or even shake a person's hand for the first time and feel "something isn't right about this dude." Whether you call it discernment or energy, it's the same cereal, different bowl.

With any type of success, there is an energy you'll emit. An aura about you begins to radiate through your pores, and the way people view/ treat you reflects on how that energy you emit translates to them, you feel me? To give you an idea, let's imagine that you've been working towards opening your own sneaker store. For some time, people have seen you stress and struggle putting your vision together. Then one day it happens, all your hard work finally pays off. Your store is up and running with customers lined up to get a glimpse of the new swanky establishment. Without you saying a word, your achievement will radiate an energy. There will be some people that say, "Wow! I saw them work so hard. They deserve it! Hey, if they did it, I can too, I gotta get cracking!" that's called inspiration. While there may be some that say, "What! Why them? Why not me? They don't deserve it as much as I do!" that's called envy.

Even if you feel you remained the same person after attaining success, people will still analyze your actions and make their own judgment. And it can range from people feeling you are now "acting funny," to people admiring your new confidence. Your energy can be interpreted as assurance or cockiness. However, the pendulum swings, just know it definitely happens.

There was a time I was so caught up in my happy little bubble because of my success, and I felt everyone would share the same feeling of bliss. My rapture blinded me from thinking my energy could possibly translate into anything negative. But then I would begin to hear random comments from some people around me like, "Just so you know, what you do really isn't that difficult, I can do the same shit if I really wanted to." I remember being caught off guard and trying to figure out the point of that type of comment. It seemed like some people would go out of their way to try to make me feel inferior and it baffled me.

I never claimed I was better or more talented than anyone. It's not like I wanted people to continuously praise me, bow to my feet, and hold me up on some golden stool because they owed me their lives for the path I carved. Dude, that's not even my style. But I would notice some people I worked with take jabs at my character, always pointing out the negative, even discrediting my efforts. I would hear, "For the record, don't ever think you GAVE me an opportunity; I really could be doing something better than this." It almost seemed like some kind of strategy. Like an outsider gave them some bad advice and suggested, "Make sure you put Flossy down just in case he gets an ego. I know how people like him get!" But it wasn't necessary. I truly appreciated everyone's role that contributed to this manifestation and did my best to show it. So why the hell would there be people focusing on telling me what they think I CAN'T do or what they feel I DON'T know? It was weird as shit; aren't we all striving to get to new levels? So why not uplift? It was like nitpicking at my supposed flaws became a sport. I would often wonder if it was pride that made some people so overly sensitive and defensive. This was one of those times I had to burn incense in my room, fall into deep thought with a cup of herbal tea, and examine the matter with an objective eye.

So, this is my thought, insecurities are way more common than we're aware of. If you really knew how some people viewed themselves, I guarantee you'd be shocked. For example, I've been intimate with women that were absolutely gorgeous and surprisingly they had self-confidence issues. As we lay butt ass naked in bed holding each other, I would hear, "So why choose me? I hate how I look. You really think I'm hot?" I would think to myself, *She's joking right? She really doesn't know how damn sexy she is???* It amazed me at how many times I found myself reassuring a woman how beautiful she was and her body was nothing short of a masterpiece.

I bring this up to show you that the people you least expect can be the most unsure of themselves and with uncertainty comes problems. An insecure mind is more susceptible to wander off into negative territory. Some people may very well translate your energy of success into intimidation because it reminds them of the risks they didn't take, what they aspire to be, but were too scared to pursue.

At times, it seemed like my character was attacked solely for the purpose of someone feeling better about themselves, and that's not uncommon. Your energy may reveal what people do or don't see in themselves. Does that give them an excuse to act like an asshole? Hell no. I just want my insight to give you a deeper understanding of why people may act the way they do. So, don't lose sleep questioning yourself, stay your course, and ride your lane. The reasons for their actions probably go beyond you.

13

True Humility Goes Deeper than Wearing a Smile and Saying "Thanks."

The concept of "being humble" has a deeper layer than what seems obvious. Firstly, I'm a proponent of someone having self-confidence. It's important to have that inner voice remind you you're destined for greatness and to keep reaching the stars when others tell you it's not possible. Hell, you wouldn't be reading this book if I listened to what people told me I couldn't do. But once your confidence becomes what I call toxic cockiness, as in genuinely feeling others are beneath you, that's when it gets sticky.

I think it's perfectly fine for someone to feel like, "I'm the shit." But I would say let your confidence be infectious to those around you. Advocate "we ALL can be the shit," as this mentality is more motivational rather than dampening. Because when a person begins to believe "I'm the shit...and the rest of you are NOT shit!" that's where problems may arise, in my opinion.

People can reach a certain level of success and become drunk with power. Their achievements make them feel as if they know more than the next man or woman. This way of thinking begins to reflect in your actions and not in a positive light either.

As a piece of advice for someone who gains success, you'll hear people loosely say, "Be sure you stay humble." But true spiritual humility goes deeper than just saying "thank you" with a smile when you receive a compliment. It's knowing that you weren't owed, but you were actually bestowed. It's understanding that there should never be a point where you feel you've learned enough. It's having a deep value, not in the materials you attain, but in the fact that you're fortunate enough to be in a position to attain them, you feel me?

As they say in show business, "Everyone can be replaced." The meaning of this quote can generally be applied to life. No matter what level of success you're on, understand it's always possible for you to be without. Yes, you can be living a fruitful life now, but once you get comfortable in the mentality of "what I have can never end, no matter what I do," you can put yourself at risk of losing it all.

They're times I'm on stage, and in the midst of performing, I'll fall into a deep appreciative thought. My body would go into autopilot mode while I contemplated. I would think to myself, "Yo, this is wild! These people spent their hard-earned money just to watch me do what I love? If I wasn't on this stage, I'd probably be doing the same thing in front of my bedroom mirror anyway."

Remember there are people out there that would kill to be in your shoes. As cliché as that phrase is, you can't take that concept for granted. Never abuse your leverage in a situation no matter how much of it you may have because it all can be taken away easier than it was given.

I've realized everyone can't handle success. I knew of people who would paint on a smile and "play humble," but were actually far from it. Their exterior was friendly, but their interior said entitlement. I've witnessed people get ahead of themselves, and it was up to the universe to humble them, and that's the hardest way to learn a lesson.

I've seen people get so comfortable in their cockiness, it affected the way they treated people. They felt it was okay to be condescending because in their head they couldn't be replaced. From the fresh-faced production assistant on set to the overnight gym custodian, everyone deserves to be treated with dignity. Being an unpleasant person is something everyone takes mental notes of. They may not remember what you say verbatim, but they'll surely remember how you make them feel.

I'm not saying to put up a kind front because there can be an underlying opportunity for you, that would be coming from the wrong place. I'm saying you can learn from everyone, just because you may be at a "higher social status" than someone doesn't make them lower than you. Moreover, the same people you look down at from your high horse will be same people you reach for on your way down if you fall.

Understand that the concept of true spiritual humility transcends just putting on a friendly exterior.

14

Communication Without Assumptions Can Stop Problems Before They Start.

You'd be surprised at how many headaches can be avoided if you're just upfront with a person, and honest about what you can or cannot do early on if not at the very beginning. Let's be realistic, does any situation really have absolutely ZERO communication issues? I would say no, but even though none of us are perfect, it's important you're aware that neglecting a minor issue can be the catalyst behind a major disaster. Telling someone what's on your mind isn't a bad thing or something you should be scared of.

It's really in your approach. For instance, say if a minor issue arises between you and a good friend that has been loyal, I wouldn't suggest approaching them the same way you would a stranger that stole from you, but hey, that's just my opinion.

Expressing how you feel isn't negative, only if you make yourself see it that way. Some people may be blunt in their address, but that doesn't have to be your approach if you choose. It can be a simple chill statement you make in a real natural conversation; it doesn't have to be dramatic. Well, whichever way you choose, just make sure you speak up. People can only respect your honesty; they can't say, "I didn't know you felt that way. You never said anything."

Don't pretend to be happy if you're uncomfortable in a situation. All this will do is build up resentment, leading you to explode, taking your anger out on someone who may have not even deserved it in that fashion. At that point, it would be YOUR fault because when they initially asked if you were okay, you said, "Yea, I'm great, everything is all good!" when you actually weren't "all good." You can't get mad at people for not reading your mind. So, speak up with honesty in a way you see fit or if you choose not to speak up, deal with the outcome sensibly and tactfully.

It's possible that you sometimes stumble on organic connections with people, where actions speak without having to say many words. You have each other's best interest at heart, and it's understood, these are invaluable relationships. I've been fortunate enough to have these kinds of connections, but they're rare. This is some unicorn type of shit. Don't assume everyone is the same because you will learn the hard way. Nevertheless, be honest about your intent and capabilities in all instances.

When you reach a certain level of success, you may become overly sensitive and feel like everyone has it out for you, but that's not always the case. If you do find yourself in a sticky situation with an individual, take a second to reflect and don't act on emotion, tap into your inner rationale and weigh it out, then ask yourself:

- What could've been avoided if I just spoke up?
- Could I have actually been the wrong one?
- Was this person ever being misleading because they saw an opportunity?

Like I said, genuine people are hard to find, so a simple miscommunication issue is not worth falling out over, especially when no one involved had bad intentions.

Personally, I've always been the type to tell a person exactly what's on my mind. If my feelings at that very moment don't come out my mouth, then you'll see it in the expression on my face. I'll say this though, on my journey, I've learned the hard way how important it was for me to be super transparent with people. My newfound success made some people overanxious of the potential; so, someone trying to find a way to attach themselves, in order to reap the benefits, wasn't uncommon. It's humanistic to desire security and the position I was in made me a likely meal ticket for future stability in people's eyes. I discovered I had to be very careful with my words because something I say casually in a conversation had a chance of being taken out of context and used against me.

I recall a time I was creating music in the studio with a fellow producer, out of excitement of what we just made, I shouted over the blaring tunes, "Dude, I love working with you! I'll figure out a way to incorporate you more into what I have going on!" He later twisted my words and said I made a verbal contract promising him a percentage of my entire company and threatened to proceed with legal action if he didn't get what he wanted. What in the hot sugary fried fucks? He went as far as to hold hostage all the music we created together as leverage against me. There are some dope songs my fans will never hear because of this. It was a cold move by him, and I was shocked to see the lengths some people would go to put a leash on me, I had no room for miscommunication.

Things were moving fast: I was averaging millions of views per video, performing in a new city every night and a bunch of other stuff; it was all fresh to me, and I just wanted to keep working. So, when someone offered me their services with a face of sincerity, I wasn't always on my toes about their motives. It would initially sound like, "No worries, Flossy! I want to do this for you and believe me, I want NOTHING in return. You have a good thing going, and I just want to contribute!" Then months later, that so-called "I want nothing in return" became "Oh, I assumed you knew I wanted $10,000 for what I did? Well, now you owe me back pay at my current rate, which is double, but I'm sure that's nothing for you, superstar☺" Trust me, it's a wack situation to be in and will have you looking pale in the face. You can feel deceived while they may feel led on. A lot headache could've been avoided if all expectations were out in the open. That way, from the very start I would've been able to say, "Nah, I'll pass on the offer, thanks anyway."

We all can get caught up in the moment, especially if you're the go-with-the-flow type, so telling you to NEVER make any kind of assumptions for the rest of your life would be pretty unrealistic, trust me, I get it. But what I am saying is, don't downplay the importance of transparency. Be clear about what your parameters are whenever you get a chance. You'll save yourself time, hair pulling, and stop problems before they start.

15

Your Level of Life Isn't Less Significant;
Everyone Has Moments of Self-Doubt

So, before you go perusing people's social media pages and admiring their lives, I want you to remember something. Showoff Sally won't post a selfie in front her home that just foreclosed and Flaunting Fred won't post a video of himself chasing the repo man as he carries away the car he failed to pay on. People are more likely to fabricate and even lie about their achievements than glorify their failures. I actually knew of a dude that would put on his best Sunday suit and take pictures in front of random buildings to look like a real-estate tycoon. He put in all that effort just for some coochie, and it sure did work, as he had a new woman every week.

In an age where people base self-importance on their amount of likes, views, and follows, people have become desperate and are willing to put on facades to gain societal approval. Now I know this is something you probably already heard on some talk show or read in some article, but the real question is, why no matter how many times it's reiterated to us, we can still find ourselves in moments of sadness comparing our lives to others? I feel the issue is deeper than someone just admiring another person's shiny new toy. I think it's because people can find themselves feeling alone in their struggles and forget how similar we actually all are as human beings and that's what causes a feeling of inferiority. Well, I'll tell you this, you are definitely not alone. You're not the only one behind on their bills or in limbo with their career or feel like they're getting old and need true companionship.

Way before the era of social media, people were still sulking on the couch, eating chocolate ice cream, watching stars on TV and asking themselves, "Why not me? What am I not doing right? What am I not doing enough of?" We all have had moments when we questioned our lives in comparison to others, so if you ever do have this moment, let that energy translate to inspiration rather than envy. Regardless, it isn't healthy to sit in that moment of comparing your journey to other people's achievements, because someone else's situation may appear to be blissful at first glance, but there may be another undertone we're not aware of. There are plenty of people going through the same things you are, so don't think how you feel is rare.

I remember being on the phone for hours with a successful friend of mine who is also in the entertainment industry. We talked about all the challenges we both faced as creators and entrepreneurs. The times we felt stagnant, the way people treated us, so on and so forth. Majority of our conversation sounded like, "You went through that too? You felt that way too? Yo, people did the same shit to you?" It was so refreshing. And not refreshing because I knew someone else suffered, but refreshing because I knew I wasn't alone in all that I went through. I was amazed how similar we both were, someone who already made it to levels I aspired to reach experienced my pain and got through it.

Understand that your financial or social status doesn't at all make you inferior to the next person. Think of your favorite celebrity right now, behind all the glitz and glam, they have emotions like any other human being, which means they're not exempt from having feelings of doubt and uncertainty. While you're sitting in your room unsure of yourself, doubting you'll ever be as rich and famous as Celebrity Sam on television, Celebrity Sam may be sitting in his mansion unsure of himself, doubting he'll ever find sincere people in his life. The fact of the matter is that everybody has his or her own issues. I'm not telling you this so you can revel in someone else's pain; I just want you to understand you're not alone in your struggles. Don't let people's external perception of "living the good life" make you feel your level of life is less significant or feel you're not important enough to inspire and spread encouragement. People have the same pressures, just different pipes. Try to find any kind of appreciation in your own obstacles. Stay your course, and as tempting as it may be, try not to play detective, investigating other people's lives, and then compare yourself. You're only setting yourself up for disappointment. Besides, you are way more fortunate than you think.

16

When It Becomes the Universe's Battle, Don't Stress Yourself Fighting. Just Stay True to Your Purpose

Ok, so you stumble across your five-year plan written on a coffee-stained sheet of paper from a few years back. You have a panic attack because even though you followed your written plan to a T, you're still not where you want to be in life. You've done everything possible, so why isn't the plan coming together? You question your life and ask yourself frantically, "What's next?!" Well, chill out hot slacks, everyone and their mama have these episodes, but I realized something. When following your passion, it's important to set goals to strive for, but don't be so married to "plans." They're nice and all, but life can always throw one hell of a curve ball to keep you on your toes.

There will be times you feel you've tried EVERYTHING imaginable and things still don't pan out as you anticipated. At that point, it's no longer your fight, it becomes the universe's battle. Does that mean your vision won't materialize? Nah, I'm not saying that at all, it just may not be on your time, you feel me?

It's completely in our control to get up off our asses and take whatever steps needed towards our passions, no excuses. That's what you call planting seeds. Now, knowing exactly when those seeds will sprout... that can be out of your hands. When you set your goals, take them for what they are, goals; achievements you will eventually attain hopefully sooner than later. But if it's later, that doesn't mean it's your fault. I know it's easier said than done because we all have anxiety attacks; but, when you learn the importance of enjoying the process, you won't beat yourself up so bad about the timing. Especially when you've done all you can.

I'd get so frustrated when I made a million phone calls along with sending a billion emails, attended countless snobby networking events, spent my last dollars to book plane tickets to take meetings with big wigs that promised to "take me to the next level" and would still get little to no results. I began comparing my style of art to others flourishing and racked my brain on ways I could possibly alter my technique. However, all my attempts ended up in a suspended state of pending, a "don't call us, we'll call you" limbo. I was exhausted and out of ideas for new strategies. But rejection made me understand it's not wise to stress over things I have no control of. And when I changed my thought process, stayed true to who I was, and just kept moving forward, I would begin to see results when I least expected it.

Sometimes the universe can even steer us in a different direction than planned, but because it's not what we originally foresaw, we surf against the tide instead of going with the flow. But the universe may be paving the road that's best for you. So don't fear to be uncomfortable, learn to adapt and adjust without losing focus of your ultimate purpose.

As I said earlier in the book, there was a point in time where I solely wanted to be a dancer, nothing more and nothing less. Dancing background on a major artist's tour would be my apex and the thought of it not happening was terrifying. My friends would often suggest I try different approaches, but my mind was set; I will keep going to dance auditions until someone "discovers me." But imagine, for years, sleeping on floors, not being able to afford meals, waiting in long cold lines for hours to be seen, and then not booking gigs because an asshole judge discriminated against your skin tone or you simply didn't know the right person in the "in-crowd." I was devastated when things weren't panning out how I pictured. But one day, I thought long and hard about it, sometimes we neglect our disguised blessings and turn our backs on alternative routes we can take that can still lead us to our ultimate goals.

After hearing the umpteenth "Nope...Next" at an audition, I started to mainly focus on honing all my crafts. I would spend hours in my room coming up with choreography and also write down song ideas whenever they came to my head, something told me one day everything would tie together somehow. As I started riding life's waves while staying true to myself, other paths began to reveal themselves like filmmaking, creating music for other artists, etc.

In hindsight, it's crazy how things panned out. I actually ended up with more than what I originally desired. It's like things came around full circle, plus a bag of chips. Not only have millions seen me dance, but I've also been bestowed a platform where I'm able to use my talents to help others. So, all those "NOs" from snobby big sunglasses-wearing, coffee-sipping judges at dance auditions was the universe's way of saying, "Don't limit yourself, there is so much more in store for you."

So, whatever your ultimate vision is, stay true to your purpose, remain focused, and keep pushing forward. Even if you feel you've done it all and nothing is working, try not to stress, just keep moving. Sometimes we think we know what's best for us, but you'll realize the universe's timing is always the most perfect. Your initial desires may be small potatoes compared to the greater plan the universe has in store for you.

Epilogue

I wrote this book with the hopes of people learning from my story. Maybe someone out there can acquire knowledge from my obstacles or be inspired by my achievements. I know I have a lot more road ahead of me, so there'll probably be plenty more times I bump my head, but I look forward to my growth. I wanted to let people know that there is hope, and if I had the heart to keep going, after all I endured, you surely can.

Sometimes society can seem so self-absorbed and so concerned about solely "doing them." It's almost as if people achieve a certain level, and because they're content, they aren't compelled to help the next man or woman. We can't become so consumed in our own wants, we neglect enriching each other, as life itself can be hard enough. You never know the obstacles someone is going through, so understand that the simplest kind word or gesture can be more impactful to another person than you think.

I want to say thank you to all my fans, family, and friends; those who support me throughout my journey. And I also give gratitude to those that didn't support me, because your doubt made me push harder. The love from my supporters means the world, words cannot express, you feel me? I will forever be appreciative. Hopefully, you gained something truly valuable from my words. Until next time...

F. Floss